WHY DO
WE LOVE
THE

Printed in the United States of America

First Edition

10 9 8 7 6 5 4 3 2 1

Library of Congress Catalog Card Number: 01-110831

ISBN: 0-7868-5334-4

Visit www.disneyeditions.com

Why Do We Love the Mouse?

by Michael Mullin

Based on the television advertising campaign
created by Dexter Fedor, Disney Consumer Products

 EDITIONS

NEW YORK

"Where do I begin?"

"He doesn't mind
if I break curfew."

"He knows you don't have to grow up."

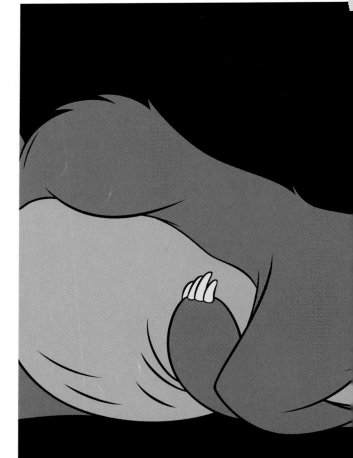

**"You just can't help
but be tickled
by the little guy."**

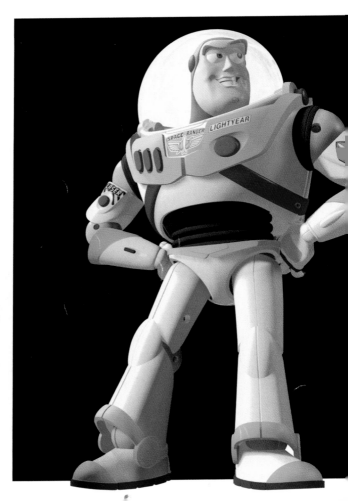

"He's got 'hero' written all over him."

"I got my reasons
and that's that."

"He can make just about anyone smile."

"He's got style.
What else is there?"

"I just do."

"I would most certainly follow *his* advice."

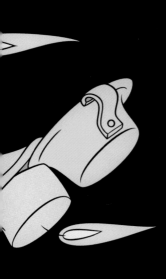

"He is a *très* welcome guest!"

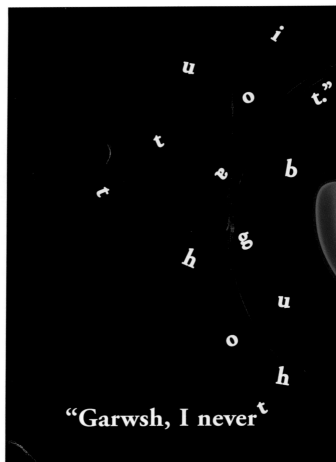

"Garwsh, I never thought about "i u o t." t b e t g h u o h

"He's deep. But
not too deep."

"He's as real as can be."

"He's rootin'.
And pretty darn
tootin', too."

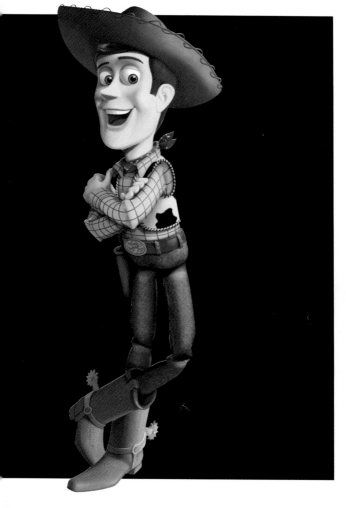

"He's very b-b-b-brave for someone his size."

"His spirit just
sorta grabs you."

"He makes life
da bubbles!"

"He lets me sleep in."

"He knows right
from wrong."

quite clever."

"He is really

"He's got energy.
I admire that."

"He is the true master
of all that is happy."

"He's the real deal."

"He gets the joke."

"He's a wonderful
little friend."

"He's hotter than hot."

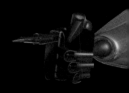

"He alone will
be spared."

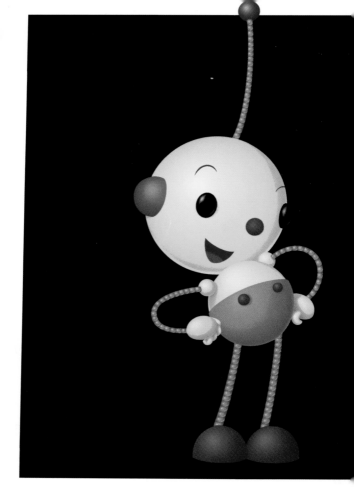

"He's okeydokey."

"He's got more spunk
than a barnful
o' critters."

"Why do I have to go LAST?!?!?"